let's Travel in

WEST

GERMANY

Edited by Fran Dyra

Claus J. Born, Manager
German National Tourist Office
Consultant

A TRAVEL PRESS BOOK

PICTURE ACKNOWLEDGMENTS

The full-color pictures in this book are the work of the following photographers, whose collaboration is gratefully acknowledged.

G. Seider (page 17); W. Schmidt (page 24); W. Benser (page 27); E. Carlé (page 28); S. Kübe (page 32); P. Reckling (page 44); M. Becker (page 47); D. Geissler (page 51); R. Hetz (page 52); S. Allan (page 59); U. Knipping (page 71) of Zentrale Farbbild Agentur, G.M.B.H., Düsseldorf; Press- und Informationsamt, Bonn (pages 20, 31, 36, 56, 67); Wolfe Worldwide Films, Los Angeles (pages 39, 48, 60, 79); German National Tourist Office, Chicago (pages 23, 72, 76); Foto Sachsse, Bonn (pages 19, 68); Archiv, V-Dia-Verlag, Heidelberg (page 40); Verkehrsverein, Bremen (page 43); Tourist Office, Cologne (page 55); Andres and Company, Hamburg (page 63); Röchling' sche Eisen- und Stahlwerke, GmbH, Völkingen/Saarland (page 64); Landeshauptstadt, Düsseldorf (page 75); F. Ganzhubner, Verkehrsamt der Stadt, Trier (page 35).

For the black-and-white photographs we wish to thank Press- und Informationsamt, Bonn (pages 8, 11, 13, 61); Tourist Office, Cologne (pages 12, 14, 26, 34); Verkehrsverein, Bremen (pages 25, 42, 73); German National Tourist Office, Chicago (pages 33, 77); Paulus Belling, Bonn (page 18); Landeshauptstadt, Düsseldorf (pages 21, 74); International Bodensee Verkehrs-Verein, Friedrichshafen (page 30); Bayreuther Festspiele, Bayreuth (page 57); Fremdenverkehrs- und Kongress-Zentrale, Hamburg (page 62). The map was made by Robert Borja.

CONTENTS

N

NORTH
SEA

BALTIC

31

24 • HAMBURG

Elbe River

14

BREMEN •

Hanover

30

16

26
• HANNOVER

21

27

East Ge

Netherlands

WEST

20
• COLOGNE

13

Belgium

• BONN

2

GERMANY

4

Luxembourg

10

FRANKFURT
AM MAIN

15

Rhine River

29

5

22

HEIDELBERG

25

12

DINKELSBUHL

Bavaria

France

28

18

Danube

BADEN
BADEN

• STUTTGART

17

3

MUNICH

Baden

1

19

7

8

23

SEA

BERLIN

many

Poland

Czechoslovakia

River

Austria

Locales of thirty-two full-page pictures

WEST GERMANY, LAND OF OLD AND NEW

THE Federal Republic of Germany—usually called West Germany—reaches from the Alps in central Europe to the Baltic and North seas. West Germany is bordered by more nations than any other country in Europe: Denmark to the north; the Netherlands and Belgium to the northwest; Luxembourg and France to the west; Switzerland to the south; and Austria and Czechoslovakia to the east. To the northeast lies East Germany, officially called the German Democratic Republic.

West Germany's landscape varies from breathtaking mountains to gentle plains, from barren heaths to fertile vineyards, from busy river ports to quiet villages, from modern cities to Roman ruins.

Lumber and wood products provide a major share of the country's economy. About twenty-eight percent of West Germany is forested. Agriculture—mostly in meat and dairy products—is very important. West Germany's greatest natural resource is coal. Potash, rock salt, and petroleum are also found. However, West Germany's primary economic strength lies in its people and its industrial development. Science, technology, and big business have been largely responsible for Germany's rapid economic growth.

9

THE PEOPLE

Although the dialects and temperaments of West Germany's sixty million people differ widely from region to region, the Germans do have certain characteristic traits. One is a deep respect for cleanliness. Houses built hundreds of years ago sparkle inside and out. Another trait—orderliness—is carried over to business and political dealings. A highly detailed report or system can always be expected from the Germans. Family is also important to the Germans, as is a deep nationalistic pride. Surrounded as it is by so many other nations, West Germany has often been involved in wars over its boundaries.

FROM THE RHINE TO THE SEAS

West Germany is made up of eleven *lander,* or states. The northernmost land is the peninsula of *Schleswig-Holstein,* washed by the North and Baltic seas. Schleswig-Holstein is a rich farming area.

Hamburg lies entirely within the boundary of Schleswig-Holstein, but it is a separate "city-state," known for its great harbor.

Further south is *Bremen,* another city-state. Like Hamburg, it has been an independent shipping center for hundreds of years.

Bremen lies within the boundary of the *land* (state) of *Lower Saxony,* which is mostly agricultural. Turnips, potatoes, grains, and fruit are the chief crops. Horses, cattle, and pigs are also raised. Here visitors will find the heath, where purple heather, juniper, and birch trees decorate the flat landscape.

The middle of West Germany is made up of four *lander: North Rhine-Westphalia,* which is the center for the iron and coal industries; *Hesse,* where the beautiful Main River flows through woodland, farm, and industrial areas; *Rhineland-Palatinate,* where vineyards flourish on the banks of the Moselle River and the Rhine River flows past dozens of castles; and the *Saar,* West Germany's newest *land,* rich in coal, iron, and steel resources.

The south is West Germany's favorite playground. In the *land* of *Baden-Wurttemberg,* the Black Forest, numerous health spas, and the *Boden See* hum with vacationers. *Bavaria,* whose people are steeped in legend, is a land of farms, lakes, and the beautiful Alps.

The eleventh West German *land* is *West Berlin,* a city-state that lies deep in the heart of East Germany. Isolated from the rest of Germany, Berlin proudly maintains its freedom and industrial success.

THE RHINE—GERMANY'S TRADEMARK

A castle round every bend; lush vineyards sloping to the water's edge; boats full of singing, happy people; a little town nearly hidden behind the trees; ancient treasure guarded by golden-haired mermaids; a busy, bustling harbor crowded with ships flying the flags of many nations. The Rhine River can be any or all these things.

The Rhine River is 540 miles long. In some places it is rough and dangerous. In other places it is gentle and quiet. All along its route, the Rhine River passes some of the most charming and breathtaking scenery in the world. Most memorable are its many castles, cathedrals, ancient cities, and vineyards. In one twelve-mile stretch of the river, there is a castle every mile!

FROM TRIBES TO A NATION

The Germanic people originally came to central Europe from Scandinavia and from the shores of the Baltic Sea. No one is quite sure when they first arrived. By 55 B.C., when Julius Caesar conquered Britain, Germanic tribes were living in several areas of Europe. Tacitus, a Roman historian, described the tall, blond people who hunted and fished and lived in tribes in his book, *Germania*. The tribes that lived in the north were called the Saxons. Those settling around the Rhine were Franks. Other Germanic tribes lived farther to the south.

Gradually these tribes settled most of the lands east of the Rhine

11

and Danube rivers. When the Roman Empire began to spread its power here, the Romans and Germanic tribes clashed. Slowly, however, an alliance grew between the two peoples. Wealthy Romans built such cities as Bonn, Trier, and Frankfurt in Germanic lands.

In A.D. 300, the Roman Emperor Constantine adopted Christianity. Soon, many of the Germanic tribes also became Christians. Then in the fifth century, a Mongol tribe from Asia, led by Attila, called the Huns, invaded Europe. For years, wars raged throughout Europe, ending when the Goths, a Germanic tribe from eastern Europe, defeated the Romans. The Roman Empire fell.

Without the power of Rome, local Germanic kings began to independently expand their kingdoms. Then Charlemagne, king of the Franks, conquered and united many Germanic tribes, converting all the people to Christianity. Soon, his empire stretched far. In A.D. 800, Pope Leo III crowned Charlemagne and proclaimd him "Emperor of the Romans." Not since the days of the first Roman Empire had there been such unity in western Europe.

After Charlemagne's death, his kingdom was divided. Once again the Germanic people were disunited. Then in the tenth century, Otto the Great successfully reunited part of Charlemagne's empire. In 962, Otto I was crowned emperor of the Holy Roman Empire. This new empire, though often weak and loosely organized, lasted more than eight hundred years.

From soaring heights, filtered light passes through the delicate, stained-glass windows of this cathedral.

In the fifteenth century, the Renaissance swept over Germany. By 1450 Johann Gutenberg had printed his famous Bible, the first to be printed with movable type. Albrecht Dürer, perhaps Germany's most famous artist, began his work. People began to read, to question old ideas, and to study new ones. The Renaissance, begun in Italy, swept Germany.

In 1517 Martin Luther, a monk, began to preach against the Catholic church's taxation and corruption. Although he was later outlawed from the church, the reform movement Luther began took root, and Protestantism was born. Soon, Luther's ideas spread to other European countries. A period of wars began as Catholics and Protestants fought for political control in Germany. In 1618, the Thirty Years' War began, and all Europe became a battlefield. When the fighting ended in 1648, all 350 German principalities had won political and religious independence. The Holy Roman Empire was from then on an empire in name only.

Amidst West Germany's ultra-modern architecture, Rathauses (*town halls*) *hundreds of years old still stand.*

It wasn't until 1804 that Germans became involved in another major war. In that year, Napoleon Bonaparte, emperor of France, began to expand his empire. Soon, much of western and southern Germany was under his power. In 1813, Prussia—one of the strongest German kingdoms—joined the Russian and Austrian armies and defeated Napoleon at the Battle of Leipzig.

The power of Prussia grew. In 1871, Germany became a nation, uniting under the Prussians. Otto von Bismarck became chancellor of the new federation of German states.

In 1888, Kaiser Wilhelm II came to power. Wilhelm feared being encircled by so many other nations. Throughout Europe, the distrust of nations for each other was leading to the forming of military alliances. Britain, France, and Russia established one such alliance. Russia and Serbia formed another. Germany, Austria, and Italy formed a third.

On June 28, 1914, an Austrian archduke and his wife were assassinated in Serbia. By July 28, 1914, Austria-Hungary declared war on Serbia. Russia and France came to Serbia's aid. Germany declared war on Russia and France. World War I had begun. By the time the war ended in 1918, it involved nations on every continent.

Germany was defeated and became a republic in 1919. Yet, it faced many problems caused by the war. Inflation in Germany was so great that a week's wages could not buy a loaf of bread. Then in 1929 a world-wide depression occurred. Conditions worsened. The Nazi party, which promised to care for the poor and make Germany a world power, began to gain members and political strength.

13

In 1933, the Nazi party's leader, Adolf Hitler, was named chancellor of Germany. But Hitler was not satisfied. He soon overthrew the government and established the Third German Empire, or Third *Reich*. Hitler's desire for power was to lead Germany into another war. On September 1, 1939, Germany attacked Poland. Again, the nations of the world took sides, and World War II began. When it ended in 1945, Germany was a bombed and leaderless nation. Under the control of the winning nations, Germany was divided into four sections. What is now East Germany was controlled by Russia, and West Germany was governed by France, Great Britain, and the United States. By 1949 France, Great Britain, and the United States withdrew, and West Germany was given its independence. East Germany adopted the communistic system and remained influenced by Russia, separate from West Germany.

RETURN TO GREATNESS

The economic growth of West Germany has been fantastic. At the end of the war, the nation was in shambles. More than two million buildings had been destroyed. Many of its cities were made unrecognizable. There was a shortage of food, an almost complete destruction of shipping and rail lines, and no federal government. Yet today, West Germany is again an economic and political power. This tremendous recovery is the result of the hard work of the German people. They have built a new nation. Once more, West German ports are crowded with ships from many nations. Once more there is an ample supply of food, beer, and wine. Modern skyscrapers stand beside restored medieval castles to typify a new West Germany, a democratic nation reborn through the love and labor of all her people.

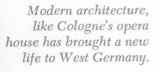

Modern architecture, like Cologne's opera house has brought a new life to West Germany.

let's travel in

WEST

GERMANY

BLACK FOREST
FARMHOUSE:
SECLUDED BEAUTY

UNDER one huge, low-hanging roof, families of the Black Forest, or *Schwarz Wald*, can perform many of their daily duties indoors, snugly protected from the icy winds of winter. The main floor of a *Schwarzwald-haus* is usually the family's living quarters. The barn housing the animals might be behind the living quarters. Frequently there is a side workshop, where during the winter the family can make cuckoo clocks, wooden toys, and musical instruments.

The hamlets and timbered houses of the Black Forest are built in a style centuries old. They are isolated by deep valleys, thick forests, still lakes, and rugged slopes of limestone and sandstone. In winter, these houses are sometimes completely snowed in. The farmers and woodsmen who live here are thoughtful and quiet, seemingly unaware of the tourist attractions that surround them. For holidays and festivals they often wear quaint, colorful costumes that have been worn for centuries: gaily colored skirts and aprons and bright, ball-round hats with wide ribbons (called *Bollenhuts*) for the women; jaunty hats and bright-buttoned jackets for the men.

The Black Forest was so named because of the density of its foliage. Thousands of tall fir, oak, and beech trees rise from green meadows. In the fall, the trees form islands of color between the hills. Mountains, streams, and open fields interrupt the forest areas. Rambling footpaths weave through the area, offering a healthy, quiet way of viewing the forest. In every season, the varied landscape irresistibly draws foreign and West German tourists alike. They come to ski in the mountains (the second highest in Germany), to fish, or to stay at one of the health resorts clustered around refreshing springs.

16

BONN:
SOFT-SPOKEN
POLITICS

ALTHOUGH Bonn has been the capital of the Federal Republic of Germany since 1949, it still has the air of a "professor-turned-politician." This is partly because, at heart, Bonn is a university community. Its university, founded in 1818, is one of the finest schools in the country. In contrast to most capitals, which reflect the hurried pace of government decision-makers, Bonn is green and leisurely with little parks and treelined streets. Even the *Bundeshaus* (Parliament) stands in calm, clean dignity along a wide promenade on the banks of the Rhine.

Typical of Bonn is its pride in the house at No. 20 Bonngasse, where the great composer, Beethoven, was born in 1770. Today, the house is a museum. Beethoven is also honored by the ultramodern concert hall bearing his name where an annual music festival is held.

Bonn was founded over two thousand years ago as a fortified Roman camp. In the thirteenth century, the Prince Electors of Cologne, who were the ruling nobles of the region, made Bonn their capital. Since that time, Bonn has been important in the history of Germany. The Palace of the Electors today serves as the main university building.

Throughout Bonn there are many statues and tributes to Ludwig von Beethoven.

Other remainders from the past are the unique *Minster*, a cruciform (cross-shaped) church with five towers, built in the fourth century; and Poppelsdorf Castle, which is surrounded by beautiful botanical gardens. The *Alter Zoll* (Old Toll Gate) offers a beautiful view of the Rhine River and of this dignified capital of West Germany.

18

CASTLES: CENTURIES-OLD ELEGANCE

ALTHOUGH many of West Germany's castles lie in ruins, weed-filled and crumbling, others stand as solidly as when they were first built. Dozens of castles have been restored and made into hotels. A stay in a castle offers visitors a chance for an elegant, romantic look into the past.

Isolated from the cities and surrounded by peaceful parks, castle hotels offer a delightful quietness. The rooms are filled with furniture from the period in which the castles thrived, adding to their authenticity. The restaurants serve fine food, and special events take place in the grand ballrooms and halls. Tennis courts, riding trails, and modern swimming pools are added attractions. Castle gardens are kept flowering and offer excellent spots for walking and resting. Although some of the castles date from the eleventh century, they are warm and comfortable. Some even have private baths and showers, luxuries no German king or court ever enjoyed!

The most magnificent castles in West Germany were built by "The Mad King," Ludwig II. His extravagances left his country near bankruptcy, but they also left much pleasure and beauty. Perhaps the most decorative of Ludwig's castles is Linderhof Palace, in the Ammergau Mountains of Bavaria. Linderhof is built in the French Rococo style. An artificial, illuminated lake, well-cared-for terraced gardens, and elaborate fountains and statues decorate the castle grounds.

This is Neuschwanstein (NOYSCH-*vahn-shtoine*) Castle, which stands in the mountain forests near Lake Alpsec in Bavaria. Built between 1869 and 1886, Neuschwanstein imitates medieval architecture. Its gloriously-shaped towers, turrets, pinnacles, and gables all soar grandly into the air.

Frederick Barbarossa's palace, built in the twelfth century, is now in ruins.

THE LORELEI:
MAJESTIC
BEAUTY

THIS colorful excursion boat on the Rhine River stops at small ports and at big cities as it picks up more and more people. Along the way, the passengers sing, laugh, and wave to passersby on the road. Suddenly, a huge rock appears ahead, filling the river and allowing little room for the boat to pass. The river twists and bends. Sharp rocks, strong currents, and shallow water make navigation so difficult that often special pilots board the boats to guide them safely past the cliff. The surf pounds against the rock's edge, pulling the boat toward it.

But, despite the danger, the passengers always greet the sight of the rock with a loud cheer and a toast. For this rock is the Lorelei, the most famous and best-loved landmark in Germany.

Covered with green shrubs, the Lorelei thrusts itself out from the right bank of the Rhine, towering over the river. In majestic beauty, it seems to guard the entrance to a land where mere mortals are no longer the rulers. From the top of this splendid rock, we can see the Rhine, twisting and bending its way past castles, vineyards, and towns.

German legends are full of spirits who live in water, earth, and fire, guarding them from human intrusion. The Lorelei, legend says, is guarded by a beautiful maiden who dwells at its top. She sits combing her golden hair with a golden comb. As the boats sail pass, the sailors can hear her. So "magically sweet and strong" is her voice that the sailors are distracted from the pounding surf and lured to the rock. They can see nothing but the beautiful Lorelei. Then, as Heinrich Heine says in his poem about the beautiful maiden:

> And lo, the wild waters are springing—
> The boat and the boatman are going . . .
> And this, with her poignant singing,
> The Lorelei has done.

WORKING IN THE VINEYARDS: HARVEST OF EXCELLENCE

ABOUT a hundred days of sunshine between May and October are needed to produce a great wine, experts say. If they are correct, the sun must shine often on West Germany for her wines are among the lightest and finest in the world.

When the grapes have been harvested, they are sent to the press house. Here they are squeezed hydraulically under waterpower and fermented in cool cellars which preserve their freshness, lightness, and pale, green-gold color. Huge casks are filled to the very top. From time to time, the casks are "racked," siphoning wine from one cask to another, leaving sediment behind. This process, which takes from six to eighteen months, results in the brilliantly clear liquid that the Germans call *abfullfertig,* or ready for the bottle.

Along the Rhine, Neckar, Main, Nahe, and Moselle rivers, hillsides and riverbanks are covered with vineyards. Each district is proud of its particular specialty, which is served in the local inns. The men, women, and children of the wine-making villages all help harvest the crop. A good harvest results in festivals throughout the wine country.

West Germany's best wines come from the deeply golden Riesling grape, which grows best on hillsides and stony ground. The Rhine and Moselle valleys particularly are noted for superb, light wines. In good weather, the winegrowers may save some vines to ripen specially for late picking. The wines from such grapes, known as *"Spätlese,"* are of such high quality that some owners keep a supply for themselves to serve proudly to their guests.

Bacchus, Roman god of wine, smiles upon the customers in this German Ratskeller.

FESTIVAL:
A TIME FOR FUN

LIKE the intricate designs on the participants' masks, West German festivals often reflect many centuries of religious or historical tradition.

The Children's Festival in Düsseldorf on the Eve of Martinmas is based on a legend handed down through the centuries. In the evening the city's children carry colorful, lighted lanterns through the streets. In the town square, the lanterns illuminate the arrival of St. Martin on horseback. As he rides into the square, a shivering beggar comes forth. St. Martin cuts his cloak with his sword, giving half to the beggar. This symbolizes the joy and goodness of sharing. When the ceremonies are completed, the children go from house to house, collecting treats from housewives wishing to join in this festival of sharing.

Some festivals have historical beginnings. Munich's *Oktoberfest*, for example, has been celebrated since 1810, when King Ludwig I of Bavaria was married. Brass bands, parades, and dances are featured, and even Munich's many, enormous beer halls can hardly hold the crowds who come to celebrate each October.

In the Rhineland, wine festivals are held everywhere. The Durkheim Festival has been held annually for more than five hundred years.

There are music festivals and industrial festivals, too. Frankfurt's Book Fair is considered the best of this kind in the world.

Traditionally, carnivals are held before Lent. The biggest and

Color and symbolism are a vital part of Cologne's street parades at carnival time.

most famous ones are held at Cologne, Mainz, Düsseldorf, Bonn, Frankfurt, and Munich. Parades and floats weave their way through the happy crowds of natives and visitors. With the first sign of music, the German's traditional reserve disappears, and young and old alike eagerly join the singing and dancing.

SKIING
IN THE ALPS:
HIGH ADVENTURE

THE majestic Bavarian Alps, which separate Bavaria from Austria, are the principal skiing area in West Germany. From late November to mid-May, skiers come by mountain railroad, cable car, and automobile to glide gaily down the highest peaks in West Germany. Colorful ski outfits flash against the snowy background. Lingering ski trails leave gentle designs on the snow-covered slopes.

Probably the most popular Bavarian ski town is Garmisch-Partenkirchen. Situated on fairly level ground, the town is surrounded by tall Alpine peaks. An Olympic ski stadium, two jumps, and a slalom course are the main features of Garmisch-Partenkirchen. There is also an enormous ice stadium illuminated at night, ski schools, bobsledding, tobogganing, and facilities for curling. Ice hockey is a favorite sport in the stadium. Throughout the ski season, contests of all kinds occur between some of the best winter sports players in the world. At the end of January, International Winter Sports Week is held.

Skiing is not the only sport in the Bavarian Alps. When winter is over, the area becomes a huge health resort. Golfing, boating, and other sport facilities, plus the sunny climate make many Alpine towns popular all year round. Sailboats prance over the many lakes. Hiking in the mountains is another favorite pastime. In good weather native Bavarians and tourists can often be seen dressed in short, jumper-like overalls called *lederhosen* and carrying knapsacks as they begin their invigorating hikes through the beautiful mountains. The biggest thrill is found when a high cliff is reached, for if the day is clear, you can see Austrian villages perched on the mountainsides across the border.

BODEN SEE:
FLOWERS
BY THE SEA

WHEN the Lord created the earth, a German legend tells us, He paused for a moment to look down upon it. Seeing how good was His creation, He let fall a tear of joy. This tear became the Boden See. Today, surrounded by forests of fruit trees, the Boden See—often called Lake Constance—is indeed a beautiful sight to behold.

The Boden See is formed by the Rhine River, beginning on the Swiss bank. The Rhine reappears as a river near the city of Konstanz. One of the largest and deepest European lakes, the Boden See has played an important role in attracting visitors to southwest Germany. The Boden See lies on the borders between Austria, Switzerland, and West Germany. The hilly, rolling land around it is densely populated with villages and towns, which seem to have been placed simply to give each villager the best possible view of the brilliant, blue water. Green and gold vineyards perch here and there on the slopes.

The Boden See is a cheerful place, where people come to swim, waterski, sail, or merely relax and look at the waters. Sometimes the

Colorful, exotic plants make the Island of Mainau seem like a vacation on a tropical island.

lake is rough, and the shouts of brave sailors fill the air. Sometimes it is quiet. Then, boats of all types sway romantically back and forth in the mild air. Many boats go to the Island of Mainau, which looks like a floating park. A lovely palace sits in the middle of the island, surrounded by flower gardens in which the densely growing tulips, hyacinths, irises, roses, dahlias, and narcissus reach for the sun. Exotic trees give the island the appearance of a beautiful, multi-hued tropical forest.

WEST BERLIN: MEMORIAL TO FREEDOM

WEST Berliners had enough rubble after the war to make a mountain. So they did. The *Insulaner*, covered with earth and planted with grass and shrubs, is a 394-foot reminder of what once happened.

Today, a few wrecked buildings can still be seen in West Berlin. But all around them rise unique, modern structures. West Berlin is becoming once again a progressive, exciting city.

Kurfurstendamm Street, known as the *Kudamm*, is aglow with neon lights at night. During the day, people crowd the outdoor cafés to sit and watch the bustle of this busy street. At the Free University, students discuss ideas that, a few miles away in East Berlin, cannot be discussed. At the Philharmonic Concert Hall, and at the many nightclubs, entertainers from all over the world perform.

West Berliners have given themselves plenty of breathing space. One-fifth of this city, West Germany's largest, is made up of parks, lakes, streams, and open spaces. So, although it lies a hundred miles within the borders of East Germany, West Berlin has become a fun-loving, pleasant city abounding in color and beauty.

Reminders of the devastating war still remain. Everywhere are French, British, and English signs marking the boundaries of the city still controlled by these three powers. The badly-damaged tower of the Kaiser Wilhelm Memorial Church, which we see here, has been left standing. It warns that war must never occur again. Another poignant reminder is Berlin's liberty bell, a replica of the one in the United States. The bell hangs in Berlin's city hall. Since it rings each noon, it is a daily reminder to both East and West Berliners that the greatest gifts on earth are those of personal freedom and national peace.

Even in this modern city, the daring design of the Congress Hall is strikingly beautiful.

PORTA NIGRA
PRICELESS
PASSAGEWAY

ROMAN ruins from before the birth of Christ can be found throughout West Germany, for the Romans did much building here. Parts of walls, gates, towers, and bridges which have withstood the wear of centuries can be seen on streets which are otherwise modern.

Perhaps the greatest single collection of Roman relics can be found in Trier, Germany's oldest city. It was settled by wandering tribes at least 1300 years before the Romans. Trier's magnificent 93-foot city gate, the Porta Nigra, is thought to be as much as 1700 years old. The remains of what was once a huge amphitheater seating thirty thousand people are also preserved in Trier.

Ancient relics are still being discovered. In 1941, a Roman mosaic floor from A.D. 200 was unearthed in Cologne. It sparkles with more than a million tiny stones. Bacchus, the Roman god of wine, gaily smiles from the center of this floor.

When the builders began Cologne's city hall in 1953, they uncovered the remains of four buildings that once were a part of a huge Roman administrative center. From its palace, Constantine the Great is believed to have ruled. These remains, more than fifteen hundred years old, have been carefully protected and preserved. Today, visitors

Wealthy Romans may once have danced on this Dionysian mosaic floor.

can go below city hall and marvel at the dimly-lit, somehow "haunted" remains of an ancient civilization.

Men have lived on German soil for a long time. At least fifty thousand years before the Romans came, Neanderthal men, one of the earliest types known, roamed the land. Their bones were discovered in the Neanderthal Valley, near Düsseldorf. In a Düsseldorf museum, visitors can see a plaster copy of these bones and displays showing how a Neanderthal family might have lived.

ARCHITECTURE:
SOCIAL CHANGE

AS Germany's national political and economic power grew in the Holy Roman Empire, the diverse states began to think in terms of "German." During this period, they developed a new style of architecture using many towers and rounded arches. Because it retains some of the features of Roman architecture, it is called *Romanesque*.

Aachen Cathedral, where Charlemagne's throne still stands, is an early example of this architectural form. The cathedral at Bamberg, built in 1003-12, is another Romanesque building. One of its many treasures is this beautiful, stone "Bamberg Rider," carved in the early part of the twelfth century.

Architectural styles reflect a country's beliefs. In the Middle Ages, religion was vitally important. The people built churches such as Cologne Cathedral to proclaim their great devotion. And so, Europe developed a new style of architecture called *Gothic*, with great pointed arches. Gothic churches were built on a grand scale and reached great heights. Large stained-glass windows gave the darkened interiors a hushed and mystical effect. Wide aisles increased the feeling of enormity in rooms which could seat thousands.

In the sixteenth century, wealthy German princes frequently built elaborate palaces, copying the *baroque* style developed in Italy. Baroque palaces, often surrounded by rigidly designed landscapes, sought splendor through complex decorations. Church interiors were brightly lit, so the detailed work on altars and the colorful wall decorations could be clearly seen. Late in the eighteenth century, baroque grew even more ornate, and became known as *rococo*. The lavishness and minute detail of rococo architecture can be seen in the King Ludwig II's costly castles.

A new architectural style called the Bauhaus was established in Weimar in 1919 by Walter Gropius, a German architect. It effectively expressed the freedom, inventiveness, and adventurous spirit of the German people. Bauhaus styles revolutionized architectural ideas throughout the western world, and formed the basis of much of today's modern architecture.

DINKELSBÜHL HOUSES: COLORFUL ANTIQUES

SOME German towns have been saved from complete destruction by extraordinary circumstances. Dinkelsbühl, in Bavaria, is one example. In 1632, during the Thirty Years' War, Dinkelsbühl was captured by the Swedish army. The children of Dinkelsbühl knelt in prayer before the Swedish commander, asking that their town be spared from pillage. A fair-haired boy caught the commander's eye. He resembled the commander's son, who had died just a few days before. Touched by the boy and the children's prayers, the Swedish leader spared the town.

Today, Dinkelsbühl's crooked streets are lined with houses that are four to five hundred years old, tinted in dozens of shades of color wash. Walls and gates from the fourteenth century still stand, as does the fifteenth century Gothic St. George Cathedral. And every July, Dinkelsbühl re-enacts the dramatic scene between the Swedish commander and the children, with the *Kinderzeche* festival.

Not far away is Rothenburg, equal in beauty and antiquity. Invaded during the Thirty Years' War by the Hapsburgs, Rothenburg was also to be destroyed. Its *bürgermeister* (mayor) went to Tilly, the Hapsburg commander, asking him to spare the town. After hearing his plea, Tilly told the *bürgermeister* that the town would be spared if he could drink a huge goblet of wine in one swallow. The *bürgermeister* did, but there was so much wine it is said he died of his effort! Each year this event is relived in the play *Der Meistertrunk* (The Master Drink), by the grateful townspeople.

Rothenburg was again threatened with destruction during World War II. The Americans planned to bomb the town. But an American who had once visited Rothenburg remembered the town's charm, and persuaded his commander to allow Rothenburg to surrender first. Once again, the town was saved.

By far the most ingenious "town-saving" was done by the women of Weinsberg Castle in 1140. The enemy, led by King Konrad III, surrounded the castle, demanding surrender. King Konrad announced that the women of the castle could leave unharmed and take with them anything they could carry in their arms. The women agreed, and soon they came out, carrying their men in their arms!

AUTOMOBILE
ASSEMBLY LINE:
PRIDE IN
DEPENDABILITY

WERE it not for the Germans, modern automobiles might look quite different. Perhaps the engine would have been in back. Or cars would run on coal or other fuel. Perhaps there would not have been an automobile at all.

In 1866, Nikolaus August Otto and Eugen Langen built the first four-cycle, internal-combustion engine. Although this engine was later improved upon, its basic idea is used in nearly every car made today. The automobile hood, too, is a German invention. The Daimler Company, a pioneer in automobile history, was the first to put the engine in front of the carriage. Then they designed the familiar hood to "cover" it.

Most importantly, two Germans well may be called the true inventors of the automobile. Gottlieb Daimler and Karl Benz, working independently, both experimented with engines using gasoline for fuel. The burning gasoline propelled the cars, and thus the first workable model of the automobile was created.

German automobiles made on assembly lines like this have become symbols of careful workmanship and engineering. Today, German cars are well-known for their dependability, sturdiness, and quality. Safety is also an important feature of a German-made car. For these reasons, West Germany is second only to the United States in motor vehicle production. And, from the number of Volkswagen "bugs," stately Mercedes-Benz, and other German-made cars seen outside of Germany, it is not surprising to find that West Germany is the largest exporter of automobiles in the world.

Germany's *autobahns* were the world's first superhighways. Since the first was begun at Frankfurt in the 1930's they have been continually improved and expanded. Today, West Germany has probably the best roads in all Europe.

BREMEN:
PROUD PORT

BREMEN carries on a tradition of maritime superiority that is hundreds of years old. The Hanseatic League, formed in the early fourteenth century, was made up of northern cities with common maritime interests, of which Bremen was one. The league provided its members with trade privileges and offered protection from pirates. For nearly two hundred years, it brought political power, commercial success, immense wealth, and independence to members. From fourteen cities, it grew to a network of well over thirty port cities.

Bremen, located on the lower Weser River, is West Germany's second largest port. Here and at Bremerhaven, the city's outer port forty miles away, hundreds of ships load and unload both day and night. Bremen's miles of wharves are covered with stacks of wool, cotton, coffee, tobacco, wood, grain, and wine from all over the world.

Only two of the Hanseatic League cities—Bremen and Hamburg—

Statues of Roland, the Knight, symbol of freedom, are found throughout the cities which once were part of the Hanseatic League.

are still independent. They are "city-states," equal in status and voting power to the other nine West German *lander*. Their senates function as both city and state governments.

Bremen no longer needs a wall to guard its freedom as it did when it was founded. So today, the ramparts of the wall form a garden which completely encircles the old city. Yet, the people have not forgotten that their freedom has lasted for hundreds of years. All hold dear the statue of Roland the Knight, which stands in the marketplace. Roland, a nephew of Charlemagne the Great, was adopted by the Hanseatic cities as the guardian of their freedom. Roland has guarded Bremen well, and he remains the symbol of a city fiercely proud of its independence and success.

BALLY
MOUSON
Imperial
HAUS DER BÜCHER
ELBEO
SPAREN
BALLY
BAYERISCHE
HANDELSBANK
SCHOKOLADE
DUDEN

FRANKFURT AM MAIN: WEST GERMAN GREETER

BRIGHTLY-lit signs reflected on rainy streets advertise the products and prosperity of West Germany. Traffic jams develop on the city streets where tall office buildings and fashionable shops cluster side by side. This is Frankfurt am Main (Frankfort on the Main), a progressive city that seldom looks to the past.

Frankfurt is an outstanding showcase of modern West Germany. Tourists who arrive at the airport—the largest in Europe—or by the many railroads, are usually impressed. No monotony will be found in the blocks of tall housing projects, decorated with flower boxes on every floor. Each building is a different color! Outward beauty is not the only outstanding feature of these colorful houses and sleek skyscrapers. Built to last, each building is solidly constructed with thick walls and solid fixtures.

Though Frankfurt lives in the present and looks to the future, its past is richly historic. The city's name reveals its beginnings—tribes of Franks found it to be the easiest place at which to cross the Main River. When the Romans came, they built a bridge and a fort. Later, Frankfurt was the site of the election and coronation of emperors of the Holy Roman Empire. The Römer, in whose halls the coronation balls were held, was rebuilt after the war. Today, one of the Römer's three buildings houses the city hall. Another carefully reconstructed building is the house of Germany's beloved writer, Johann Wolfgang von Goethe (*GER-ta*).

Frankfurt was the home of many famous men. Gutenberg set up a shop here, and a newspaper was published in Frankfurt as early as 1548. The Rothschild family began building their banking fortune when they opened a small bank here. Frankfurt was also the birthplace of the atomic scientist Otto Hahn, and the city where Paul Ehrlich developed the theory of wonder drugs.

Frankfurt has given much to its nation in the past. Today, it continues this tradition of national importance by encouraging even greater economic and cultural accomplishments.

FARMER
IN THE FIELDS:
A JOB FOR
EVERYONE

BUSY harbors and bustling cities are only a part of West Germany. Two-thirds of the German people still live in rural areas. Some live in logging towns, cutting and processing trees for the lumber industry. Others live in fishing villages, catching the herring, cod, and perch needed to feed themselves and their country. Many are farmers who live in houses overlooking pleasant green valleys.

West German farms are usually small. The work is done by the farmer, his wife, and his children. Outside help is seldom hired. This farmer is using a cow to pull his plow. However, most farmers use modern farm equipment. Farm children help in the fields, milk the cows, and feed the animals. The girls also help their mothers care for the house and garden.

Eighty-six percent of the land area in West Germany is used for agriculture. The south abounds with colorful fruit orchards. In the valleys of central West Germany, grain, fodder plants, potatoes, and sugar beets are grown. The hilly lands of central and northern West Germany are devoted to livestock. Cattle, pigs, and poultry are the most important products.

For farmers and their guests mealtime is a special treat. Visitors soon learn why West Germany is known for hearty, plentiful foods. *Brätwurst* (BRAAHt-VOORST), a spicy sausage, and *knodel* (KNOH-*del*), a juicy dumpling, are universal German favorites. Bavarian farmwives may serve *brätkartoffeln* (BRAAHt-*kahrr*-TOFF-*eln*), fried potatoes. In Hesse, many dishes are smothered in *grün sosse* (GRUHN-ZOH-*seh*), a spicy green gravy. In the north, a favorite dessert is *röte grüetze* (ROHT-GRUT-*seh*), a delicious raspberry pudding served with whipped cream. Another popular treat is the delicious butter-and-almond cookies shaped like windmills. No matter where a visitor goes in Germany he can have a meal fit for a king.

FOLK COSTUMES:
A PROUD
TRADITION

THE traditional costume in the land of Hesse for farm women was a long, black, accordion-pleated wool skirt. This was worn over white petticoats and heavy white stockings. The men wore loose-fitting pants and durable plaid shirts for their work in the fields. Today, modern fashions are worn throughout West Germany. During special festivals, the men of Hesse might wear their traditional outfit. First they wrap colorful scarves around their necks. Over the scarves they wear long, loose frock coats. To complete their outfit, they wear beautifully embroidered hats. The women also have a traditional dress. They wear pretty, soft skirts, embroidered belts and bodices, and multi-colored pillbox hats.

In Bavaria, *lederhosen* are still in style. Most popular are the short leather pants, but *lederhosen* can also be worn gathered below the knee like knickers. In Bavaria on festive occasions, short pants, made of velvet or some other fine material, are often worn. This man is wearing short pants, which are decorated with sparkling leaves and appliqued designs. His jaunty hat is decorated with a *gamsbart*, a switch made of mountain goat whiskers! The woman's apron and shawl is a traditional outfit throughout West Germany. The skirt may be made of cotton, printed with animals, trees, and other folk art symbols, or of soft wool. Underneath the shawl, the blouse is likely to have embroidered, puffed sleeves and a deep, gathered neckline.

In modern West Germany folk costumes are worn only for special costume festivals or parades. Most of the people, whether they live in towns or in cities, wear the latest fashions. But West Germans, confident of their future, proudly preserve and frequently wear these symbols of their historic past.

49

STUTTGART MARKETPLACE: PLEASANT SHOPPING

NEATLY arranged under colorful striped umbrellas or canvasses, goods of all kinds await inspection on market day. Clothing stalls, sausage stalls, sweets stalls, and vegetable stalls are set up on a certain day of the week in the central squares of cities, towns, and villages across Germany. Since so many people live in rural areas, market day is the time for families to come to town to sell their wares and buy the things they need. It is also a time to see friends and catch up on the latest news.

For children, the marketplace is a myriad of colors and smells and sounds. There are the sounds of scales clattering and paper bags being filled with goods. There are brightly-colored flowers, clothing, and toys to look at and admire. There are the irresistible smells of candies, cakes, cheeses, and countless other mouth-watering treats.

Women carefully examine articles, assuring themselves of the quality. Men balance bags of goods in their arms. All around there is a feeling of cozy abundance. When it is time for a rural family to head home, there are many things for them to remember and to talk about.

Even West Germany's big cities have market days. This one, in Stuttgart's Schillerplatz, specializes in vegetables and flowers. Of course, marketplaces are not necessary in big cities, where people can shop in a variety of modern stores. Yet, it is more fun to shop in the open, where the smells of the different foods mix together enticingly in the wind, and colors seem to cheerfully glow in the bright daylight.

MUNICH
BEER GARDEN:
A TIME FOR
FRIENDSHIP

DURING the Oktoberfest, Munich's breweries erect huge beer halls. Thousands of people can be seated in each temporary hall. Bavarian brass bands provide the music. When the songs are familiar, the audience sings loudly. Countless mugs of specially prepared *Marzenbier,* beer brewed in March and aged for extra strength, are poured. A steady sound of laughter, singing, and pleasant talk fills the air as the celebrators enjoy the products which have made Munich the beer capital of West Germany.

Oktoberfest and the giant beer halls are soon gone, but some of the enjoyment continues all year in the beer halls and beer gardens found throughout Munich.

When the weather is good, customers are served in the garden and courtyard, where flowers, statues, and gay umbrellas add a festive atmosphere. In winter, or when the weather is wet, the beer drinkers fill the numerous rooms attached to the main hall. Brass bands move from room to room, playing merry folk tunes. Often, there is room for dancing. Enormous *bierkruges* (mugs), clay steins, or lidded pewter mugs are filled with the famous Bock beer. With it, many people like to eat little white sausages. If they are hungrier, they will find the meals as bountiful as the portions of beer.

Bright-colored tables fill each room. When the garden or hall is crowded, it is customary for people to sit wherever there is room. Strangers laugh and sing together, and friends happily relax after a day of hard work.

Good food, fashionable stores, and first-class theater and musical performances are trademarks of this capital city of Bavaria, for Munich is the largest commercial center in southern West Germany. But Munich's biggest charm is the friendliness of its people. Conversation flows easily, and many a person can recall a friendship that began over beer and sausages.

COLOGNE CATHEDRAL: SYMBOL OF SPIRIT

AFTER World War II, most of Cologne lay in ruins. In the midst of the rubble stood Cologne Cathedral, damaged but not destroyed. So famous was this structure that the British and American pilots who bombed the city were given this order: "Don't bomb the Cathedral."

Though the Cathedral stood at the war's end, it took over eleven years to repair the damage. It was worth it. The vast interior of this fine Gothic Cathedral includes seven chapels. Valuable religious objects adorn the church. In the Cathedral Treasury, there is goldsmith work, vestments, and utensils. The greatest treasure of all is the golden, high altar behind which are said to lie the remains of the Three Wise Men who brought gifts to Bethlehem.

Cologne is steeped in the past. And the remembrance of its heritage, which can be symbolized by the Cathedral, was what caused the fervent, dedicated desire of the Germans to "start all over again."

Today, the rebuilt city features shining housing projects, a modern opera house and city hall, and efficient, up-to-date communications facilities. Yet, the Cathedral, with its 510-foot spires, outshines them all and dominates the city's skyline.

In 38 B.C., Colognia (which in Latin means, "The Colony") was an important Roman crossroads town. Roman walls, gates, and towers have survived and stand as reminders of this city's history. Cologne's position on the Rhine River kept it prospering through hundreds of years of war and disasters. It is still the leading economic and traffic center. Eau de Cologne, a type of scent used by women the world over, has made the city a household word. However, hundreds of other items are also made in this banking, insurance, and industrial capital.

VIOLINS:
A MUSICAL
HERITAGE

BRIGHTLY-varnished violins and cellos fill this workshop. They were made by sure, deft fingers, trained in the art of making instruments that are both sensitive and rich in resonance. In the seventeenth century, a violin maker named Mathias Klotz brought the secrets of his craft to the town of Mittenwald. Since then, Mittenwald's craftsmen have become world famous as makers of musical instruments.

The notes of these violins and other instruments are heard throughout West Germany, for this nation has a rich musical heritage. Bach, Beethoven, Brahms, Mendelssohn, Wagner, and countless other composers filled Germany with music, and their echoes still ring clearly. A symphony, an opera, a beer garden brass band—all are a vital part of the music of West Germany.

Music is an intrinsic part of German life. Craftsmen even put music into many of their patiently-carved handicrafts, such as the enchanting Bavarian music box. Across the tops of these boxes, tiny carved figurines drift to the chiming rhythm of lovely tunes.

Even more familiar are Black Forest cuckoo clocks. They are shaped like the peaked-roof homes of the forest. Various animals, people, trees, and flowers are carved on the outside. Iron pinecones are used for the hanging weights. At the proper time, the cuckoo pops out of the attic window, utters his piercing, ridiculous cry, and then returns to the comfort of his delightful home.

Germans have been carving wooden clocks since the sixteenth century. In the spring, these clocks were sold to traveling peddlers, who showed their wares from house to house throughout Europe. In 1880, the cuckoo was added. So popular are these clocks today that the parts and frames are made in factories in order to produce them in large enough numbers. But the figures that give the clocks their charm are still hand-carved by the farmers and foresters of the Black Forest.

In the Festspielhaus *he designed in Bayreuth, Richard Wagner's operas are performed each summer.*

HEIDELBERG: CITY OF ROMANCE

HEIDELBERG is a city of romance. Vineyards, flowers, and trees bloom in this city which sits snugly between green hills on the banks of the Neckar River. The little city is so cozy that everything seems to run into, or come from, the narrow Hauptstrasse, a street which runs parallel to the river.

So lovely is Heidelberg that Sigmund Romberg used the city as his setting for *The Student Prince*. The inns to which the students in his opera march "under fruit trees arching" are still gathering places for students. The old bridge which spans the Neckar was built in 1786, and the Gothic Church of the Holy Ghost is a fourteenth century treasure. But nothing in Heidelberg equals its castle, the largest such ruin in Europe, which exhibits fine examples of Gothic, Renaissance, and baroque architecture.

Built between the thirteenth and seventeenth centuries, Heidelberg Castle was the residence of the Palatinate Prince Electors. Its partially-restored red sandstone buildings are grouped around a large courtyard, so that their appearance is one of a little medieval town. In the cellar is a wine vat which holds forty thousand gallons of wine. So large is the vat that a dance floor has been built on top of it! Festival plays are performed on the beautifully terraced castle gardens, and fireworks begin their flight from the castle grounds whenever there is reason for jubilation. Every night, the massive castle ruins are illuminated. Glittering in the darkness like a fairy palace, the castle completely dominates the city from its hillside perch.

OBERAMMERGAU PASSION PLAY: KEEPING A PROMISE

EVERY ten years, the Bavarian town of Oberammergau keeps a promise it made in 1633. At that time, the town was stricken by the Black Plague. The grieving townspeople promised to present a passion play—the story of the crucifixion—once every ten years if the plague ended.

Their prayers were answered. True to their vow, the townspeople have presented the Passion Play every decade in the year ending in zero. Today their play is more than a performance. It is an act of faith enjoyed and awaited by people from all corners of the world. The play is the most important event in the lives of the townspeople, for all 1250 roles are played by one of them. To assign the parts a local election is held about six months before the play. Then the players begin their preparations. Some must grow beards for their roles. Others must sew the costumes.

Visitors may wish the play was presented more often. For these deep-Oberammergau find one performance a decade enough. For these deeply religious people put all they can into the play. As a result, their performance is professional or, perhaps, *more* than professional. The re-enactment of Jesus' life and death is almost painfully and intensely alive.

Between performances, townspeople do not forget their deeply-felt faith. Religious statues, carved from wood, are made in the homes. Even the outside walls of the houses are painted with religious scenes. The House of the Passion Play remains open to visitors, and stage settings and wardrobes are displayed. One can almost imagine the play itself. But nothing can replace the thrill, the tenderness, and the compassion displayed every decade by the people of Oberammergau who have made the Passion Play their lives.

Intricate, delicate wooden sculptures are lovingly created in Oberammergau.

HAMBURG:
CITY OF WATERS

TO Hamburg, water represents both business and pleasure. The Elbe River, which flows through the heart of the city, makes Hamburg the largest seaport in Europe. Like nearby Bremen, Hamburg was a member of the powerful Hanseatic League, and it still retains its independence as a city-state. This beautiful German Renaissance building is its city hall, which houses both the city and state governments.

Now and then, a shining new ship appears on the Elbe, for Hamburg, West Germany's second largest city, is also a great shipbuilding center. Many an ocean liner's maiden voyage began when its hull slipped gently into this busy river.

Like most port cities, Hamburg has a lively night life. On the Reeperbahn, neon lights flash through the night as seamen celebrate their return to land.

Hamburg citizens turn to different waters for relaxation: its two Alster lakes. The Inner Alster, in the heart of Hamburg, is surrounded on three sides by tall, closely-built buildings. On the far banks of the larger Outer Alster, lovely, expensive villas have been built. Charming parks, including the famous Planten un Blomen botanical gardens, are located nearby. Wide promenades border the lakes, offering pleasant

Like all seamen, these sailors enjoy their shore leave.

views of the yachts and sailboats that flit across the calm waters. The Elbe River may have made Hamburg a prosperous city, but it is the Alster lakes which make it an enjoyable place to live or visit.

So much water flows through Hamburg that it has over thirteen hundred bridges. This water has also made the soil on which the city is built very marshy, so that its buildings must stand on "piles"—huge tree trunks rammed solidly into the bedrock. The city hall, for example, sits on four thousand piles!

COAL AND STEEL:
WEST GERMANY'S
SALVATION .

THE Ruhr Valley, which centers around the area where the Ruhr River flows into the Rhine, is the industrial heart of West Germany. It provides the country with its life's blood—millions of tons of pig iron, crude steel, and desirable grades of coal. The Ruhr Valley has made West Germany the third largest industrial producer in the world. It produces ninety-three percent of the coal and eighty-three percent of the steel.

Essen is the center of the Ruhr's industrial complex. Huge chemical plants and electrical and engineering concerns are located here, close to their sources of supply. Modern factories, coal mines, and blasting furnaces make up Essen's large, throbbing community, which is alive day and night. Always, the sky is reddened by the flames from open hearths and the lights of factories. Busy harbors and crisscrossing railroad tracks carry Essen's products to faraway places.

Coal and iron industries are also found in the Saar, which has been a *land* since 1957. The skyline of Saarbrücken, the capital city, is dotted with factories. At night, sparks flicker brilliantly in the darkness.

Despite West Germany's active foreign trade, much coal and steel is used at home. New buildings, metal products, and automobiles are made from West German steel. Coal is used by the country's engineering and transportation industries.

The success of West Germany's economic comeback is shown in its employment rate. In order to lower the number of unfilled jobs, millions of workers from Italy, Spain, Greece, Turkey, and many Asian and African countries have been imported. Many immigrants work in the Ruhr area, because the work week is shorter and the pay higher than anywhere else in Europe.

65

HANNOVER FAIR: SHOWPLACE OF PROGRESS

FOR nine days each year, toward the end of April, Hannover takes on an international air. In the lobbies of hotels, visitors hear languages from all over the globe. Over half a million people come to the city for the International Industrial Fair, the biggest and most important fair of its kind in the world. The appreciative ooh's and aah's of the visitors, no matter what language they speak, greet the more than five thousand exhibits which display the wealth and brains of the world.

Hannover itself exhibits locomotives, automobiles, and rubber goods, for the capital of the *land* of Lower Saxony is a busy industrial center. Other displays show models of machinery run on nuclear power. From all over the world modern advances in photographic equipment, iron and steel products, oil pumps, and office equipment will be demonstrated for eager buyers. There will even be glittering jewelry displays, shining silver place settings, and delicately designed glassware and china.

In the open spaces around the twenty-six exhibition halls, towering pieces of equipment too large to fit into even the largest of the fairgrounds' buildings are erected. Also available to trade fair visitors are lectures and speeches given by industrial leaders from many nations. Special forums to discuss industrial problems are held. Perhaps, from these discussions between educated men of many nations, an even better product emerges that will be exhibited at the next Hannover Industrial Trade Fair.

The fair also offers hungry visitors a wide choice of restaurants. Over three thousand cooks, chefs, and waiters stand ready to prepare and serve an international variety of foods.

UNIVERSITIES: SEARCHING FOR NEW IDEAS

WEST Germany, as a nation, places a high value on education. Its past is filled with scientists, inventors, and men of arts and letters who are known and admired throughout the world. Since the sixteenth century, German scientific, mathematical, and philosophical writings have been eagerly studied by scholars throughout the world. German operas and books have been translated into every language.

Today, West Germany's children start school at the age of six. They go until they are eighteen. In many cities and towns, the schools are fine, modern architectural structures. In the larger schools, the gymnasium, complete with swimming pool, is in a separate building. Wide expanses of lawn surround the buildings of steel, glass, or colorful concrete. Abstract murals and paintings adorn the hallways.

Inside the classroom, "Herr Professor," as has always been the case, rules supreme. His authority is seldom doubted. In the elementary school, the children busily study such subjects as foreign languages, history, and science. Boys and girls in West Germany have a heavy school schedule. They go to school six days a week. Their day ends in early afternoon, but there is always much homework to do.

The aim of all German students has always been to go to the university. So well respected are these schools that their enrollments include students from many other nations. On the Bonn University campus modern buildings mix with buildings which have stood for hundreds of years. This beautiful building was once the palace of the Prince Electors.

In West Germany, as in most countries, the university professors are not just teachers. They also study and learn. Research is considered as important as class lectures. What these scholars discover is of value to their students, of course. But it is also of value to the world.

BADEN-BADEN: ELEGANT REST

YOU don't have to be sick to enjoy a West German health spa. In these delightful resorts, where the healing springs compete with gambling casinos for popularity, all you need is the desire for a change of pace.

The Romans were the first to recognize the healthful qualities of Germany's many springs. Today, they are most popular with sufferers of respiratory and rheumatic ailments, who come to drink, inhale, swim, or bathe in the hot, mineral or radioactive springs at over two hundred health spas. Another reason for the spas' great popularity is the privacy they provide. Many of the health spas do not allow motor traffic. And there are quiet lanes, gardens, beaches, and meadows where guests can sit or stroll.

One of the most famous health spas is Baden-Baden in the Black Forest. In the nineteenth century, Baden-Baden was a fashionable salon, where royalty and the rich gathered. Stately elegance has remained a way of life at this spa. Superb cuisine, champagne, and music at dinnertime are added luxuries enjoyed by all the guests who come to Baden-Baden.

Beautiful gardens separate the buildings and houses from the sidewalks of the main parkway, which ends at the impressive front porticoes of the grand casino. The French-style interior of the casino, glittering with the brilliance of chandeliers, seems like a royal palace.

For the athletic, there are hiking trails, swimming pools, and fishing and skiing facilities. For those who wish to be entertained, many spas provide professional orchestras and drama companies. At Baden-Baden however, one of the favorite spectator sports is horse racing at the colorful racetrack.

PIED PIPER PLAY: TALES FROM LONG AGO

A reedy toot is heard, and the legend of the Pied Piper is re-enacted each summer at Hamelin's *Rattentagner*. First come children dressed as rats, scampering and dancing to the lilting music. Then, the Piper comes into view, dressed in a multi-colored cloak and curly-toed shoes. Following behind him are the children of Hamelin, happily imitating the Piper's movements. He leads the children through an opening in the hill which has miraculously appeared. Then, the opening closes, and the Piper and the children are never seen again.

There is some truth to the legend of the Pied Piper. Hundreds of years ago, Hamelin did lose many of its children. They might have been victims of a plague, or perhaps they perished in one of the Children's Crusades to the Holy Land. But the legend of the Pied Piper as set down by Robert Browning provides a happier ending, for the Piper is said to have led the children to a happy land.

Folktales have been told in Germany for hundreds of years, but were it not for the Grimm brothers, they might not be recorded today. Jacob and Wilhelm Grimm traveled through the Rheinhardswald Forest, listened to the age-old stories, and wrote them down. Perhaps, like the Pied Piper story, some were based on fact. People who live in the Rheinhardswald will tell you that the handsome prince awoke Sleeping Beauty in Sababurg Castle, and that Little Red Riding Hood did, indeed, live in the forest. True or not, the tales of princesses and ogres, giants and fairies, golden eggs and talking animals are rich in a color, a language, and an excitement that, for generations, have made children of all ages believe.

Statues honoring the Bremen Town Musicians are found throughout West Germany.

JAN WELLEM STATUE: BELOVED RULER

THE people of Düsseldorf are extremely proud of their statue of Johann Wilhelm II, which stands majestically in front of the town hall. The former-Elector Palatine who ruled this city on the Rhine was so loved that his subjects called him simply "Jan Wellem."

Jan Wellem has a splendid view of his busy city. Because Düsseldorf is the capital of the *land* of North Rhine-Westphalia, there are many interesting people to see: laughing university students, busy manufacturers, and visitors. But none are more delightful than the young boys who, for the benefit of passersby and a penny, turn cartwheels up and down the broad avenues.

Boys have been turning cartwheels on the streets of Düsseldorf for hundreds of years. It is so much a part of the city's tradition that the schools teach the art of *radschlagen* (cartwheel turning) in gym classes throughout the state.

According to legend, when Jan Wellem married, the entire city came out, dressed in its best, to cheer the wedding procession. As the

Düsseldorf's delightful custom is immortalized in this lifelike statue.

king and his bride waved to their subjects, one of the wheels of the carriage suddenly broke. A boy ran to the carriage. Putting his thumb in the hub of the wheel, and turning cartwheels with his free hand, the boy served as a wheel. The carriage triumphantly and safely carried the happy bride and groom to their palace.

Every August, the time the youthful cartwheelers dream of all year, the annual Radschlaeger competition is held. A prize is awarded by the mayor to the boy who does the best cartwheels. But even more important to the winner are the admiring glances he will receive all year from the other cartwheelers.

BALTIC BEACH: NORTHERN HOLIDAY

THESE shifting, sand-dune beaches are in West Germany's northernmost *land,* Schleswig-Holstein. Though the peninsula is bordered on the west by the chilly North Sea and on the northeast by the Baltic Sea, its coast is protected from the sharp winds by the lay of the land, and by thick trees and high cliffs. Even so, the large wicker-basket seats popular with sunbathers must be placed in craters dug in the sand to keep them from toppling over when gale winds blow. When the wind comes, all are reminded that despite the resort atmosphere they are indeed in the far north.

Deep green pine trees run down to the white beaches from startling red cliffs. Sailboats and water skiers on the blue waters stand out sharply and clearly in the crisp air. The result is a montage of color and fun that, in the late summer months, draws thousands of vacationers and health seekers to the beaches.

Off the coast in the North Sea are the Frisian and other small islands, inhabited by fishermen and farmers who have built dikes to hold back the sea's fierce waves. Resorts have been built on some of these islands. One of the most popular is Helgoland, whose red sandstone cliffs rise menacingly on one side but slope off to a friendly, white beach on the other. At one time, Helgoland was a shelter for sea pirates. Toward the end of World War II, the residents of Helgoland were evacuated, and the island was used by the British for target practice. Its buildings were completely destroyed. Today, the newly-built houses and resorts, painted in pastel blues and pinks, enchant thousands of visitors.

Helgoland's sandstone cliffs welcome visitors to this interesting resort island.

THE WALL: BERLIN'S HEARTACHE

EAST and West Berliners are one family, despite the political differences of the two parts of Germany to which they now belong. Once West Berliners could freely cross the border to visit friends or relatives. East Berliners could go to work or school in West Berlin. Despite two names and governments, Berlin is Berlin.

Life is better in West Berlin: entertainment is livelier, food is more abundant, wages are higher. So each year a quarter of a million East Berliners moved to West Berlin.

Then on August 13, 1961, Berliners awoke to find the beginnings of a wall separating the city. It was built by the East Berlin government to keep its people from leaving. East Berliners could no longer work in or even visit their families in West Berlin. West Berliners could no longer go to East Berlin. For the first time since their city had been divided after World War II, Berliners felt divided.

East Berlin workmen and police continued to strengthen the wall. Today, twenty-eight miles of solid concrete topped with barbed wire crosses the middle of the city. Buildings on the east side of the Wall have been emptied, their doors and windows sealed off. People who had once smiled out their windows at their next-door neighbors now see only the Wall. Streets that once wound through both sections are now dead ends.

Only authorized people can pass through the heavily-guarded Wall checkpoints. On the East German side, huge spotlights flood the area, and troops of police stand guard, guns in hand, to be sure no one climbs over the Wall. Now and then, a shot is heard. Or a scream.

Recently, the East Berlin government has allowed West Berliners to visit their families and friends in the East on certain holidays. While this is a comfort, it is not enough. For every morning, when Berliners awake, the Wall is there, zigzagging crasily along the uneven border, separating people and streets and houses which were not meant to be separated. Daily the West Berliners hope a way will be found to rid their city of what they call "The Wall of Shame."

SOME FAMOUS NAMES IN GERMAN HISTORY

ATTILA THE HUN (406?-453)—*King of the Huns who was known as "the Scourge of God." His army terrorized Europe for twenty years.*

CHARLEMAGNE (724-814)—*King of the Franks known as Charles the Great or Charles I. He conquered and united many Germanic tribes, converting many to Christianity. Crowned "king of the Romans" in 800, he laid the foundations for the Holy Roman Empire.*

JOHANN GUTENBERG (1400?-?1468)—*Inventor of printing using movable type. He used this method to print the first Bible (the Gutenberg Bible).*

MARTIN LUTHER (1483-1546)—*Monk who preached against the Catholic church's taxation and corruption. The reform movement he began became widespread, and Protestantism was born.*

JOHANNES KEPLER (1571-1630)—*German astronomer who discovered three laws on the motion of the planets, known as Kepler's Laws.*

GEORGE FREDERICK HANDEL (1685-1759)—*Composed operas, odes, church and chamber music. He was best-known for* The Messiah.

IMMANUEL KANT (1724-1804)—*Transcendental philosopher and writer.*

JOHANN WOLFGANG VON GOETHE (1749-1832)—*German poet who greatly infllenced drama and literature in Germany.*

LUDWIG VON BEETHOVEN (1770-1827)—*Germany composer whose symphonies introduced new musical forms.*

JACOB (1785-1863) and **WILHELM** (1786-1859) **GRIMM**—*Librarians and writers. Their most famous, popular work is* Grimm's Fairy Tales.

FELIX MENDELSSOHN (1809-1847)—*A pianist and conductor as well as a composer of symphonies. His oratorios include* St. Paul *and* Elijah.

RICHARD WAGNER (1813-1883)—*Operatic composer, philosopher, and poet. Most of his operas were based on German myth and legend. His operas include* The Flying Dutchman, Lohengrin, *and* Tristan and Isolde.

PRINCE OTTO LEOPOLD VON BISMARCK (1815-1898)—*Prussian statesman who became the first chancellor of the German Empire. Known as "the Iron Chancellor," his political, economic, and social policies strengthened the empire.*

FRIEDRICH NIETZSCHE (1844-1900)—*Philosopher and writer whose theories about mankind were to be misunderstood, and were said to have influenced the Nazi's social and political philosophy.*

WILHELM CONRAD ROENTGEN (1845-1923)—*German physicist who discovered X rays. He was awarded the Nobel prize for physics in 1901.*

KAISER WILHELM II (1859-1941)—*Emperor of Germany and King of Prussia, who began the industrialization of Germany. Germany's last monarch.*

THOMAS MANN (1875-1955)—*Novelist, who received the Nobel prize for literature in 1929.*

ALBERT EINSTEIN (1879-1955)—*Theoretical physicist and mathematician whose theory of relativity revolutionized scientific thinking about space, time, gravitation, matter, and energy. His formula, $E=mc_2$ (Energy equals mass x velocity of light squared), was used to work out some of the basic problems of atomic energy. He was awarded the Nobel prize in 1921.*

ADOLF HITLER (1889-1945)—*Leader (Führer) of the National Socialist (Nazi) Party. Hitler's invasion of Poland, in 1939, brought on World War II.*

SOME IMPORTANT DATES IN GERMAN HISTORY

98 A.D. *Tacitus'* Germania *describes Germanic tribes settled in central Europe.*

312 *Roman Emperor Constantine adopts Christianity. Many Germanic tribes are converted to this religion.*

375 *Huns invade Europe. Germanic tribes seek shelter in Rome.*

501 *Clovis I, king of the Franks, establishes an empire.*

800 *Charlemagne, king of the Franks, is proclaimed "Emperor of the Romans." Germanic tribes united into a Christian empire.*

962 *Otto I crowned emperor of the Holy Roman Empire, which lasts until 1806.*

1358 *Under the leadership of the port city of Lübeck, north German cities form the Hanseatic League.*

1450 *Johann Gutenberg printed his famous Bible using movable type.*

1517 *Martin Luther begins preaching and the Protestant Reformation begins.*

1618-1648 *Thirty Years' War between Catholics and Protestants seeking political and religious control involves most of Europe.*

1648 *Treaty of Westphalia, ending the Thirty Years' War, gives all religious groups the right to worship as they choose.*

1806 *Napoleon invades Germany and dissolves the Holy Roman Empire.*

1813 *Napoleon defeated at Battle of Leipzig. Germany freed from French domination.*

1871 *Germany becomes a nation. The Prussian Otto von Bismarck is named chancellor of the new state.*

1914-1918 *World War I. Germany, Austria, and their allies are defeated. Kaiser Wilhelm II is sent to exile.*

1919 *Under Weimar Constitution, Germany becomes a democratic republic.*

1933 *Adolf Hitler appointed chancellor of Germany.*

1939-1945 *World War II. Nazi Germany defeated.*

1949 *Federal Republic of Germany is established by the governments of France, Great Britain, and the United States. The Soviet Union keeps control of the eastern section. West Germany is politically divided from East Germany.*

1961 *East Germany erects a wall between East and West Berlin.*

1969 *Willy Brandt becomes Chancellor.*

SOME GERMAN WORDS AND PHRASES

Do you speak English?	Sprechen sie Englisch? (SHPREC-*en* ZEE ENG-*lish*)
Can you help me?	Konnen sie mir helfen? (KOH-*nen* ZEE MEER HELF-*en*)
I do not understand.	Ich verstehe nicht. (IC *fer*-SHTEH NICT.)
What do you wish?	Was wünschen sie? (VAHSS VUNSH-*en* ZEE)
Thank you	Danke (DAHNGK-*a*)
Please, You are welcome	Bitte (BITT-*a*)
How much is it?	Wieviel kosten das? (*vee*-FEEL KOST-*en* DAHS)
Why?	Warum? (*vah*-ROOM)
What?	Was? (VAHSS)
Who?	Wer? (VAIR)
When?	Wann? (VAHNN)
Yes	Ja (YAAH)
No	Nein (NIYN)
Perhaps	Vielleicht (*fi*-LIYCHT)
Good day	Guten tag (GOOT-*en* TAAHG)
Goodbye	Lebewohl (LEHB-*e*-VOHL, Auf Wiedersehen (*owf* VEE-*der-zehen*)
Where is it?	Wo ist? (VO IST)
Ladies' room	Damen (DAA-*men*)
Men's room	Herren (HERR-*en*)
Airplane	Flugzeug (FLOOK-*tsoyk*)
Airport	Flughafen (FLOOK-*haahfen*)
Bus	Autobus (OW-*to-booss*)
Train	Zug (TSOOK)
Boat	Boot (BOHT)
Baggage	Gëpäck (*gha*-PEK)
Hotel	Hotel (*ho*-TEL)
Station	Bahnhof (BAAHN-*hohf*)

DAYS OF THE WEEK

Monday	Montag (MOHN-*taahk*)
Tuesday	Dienstag (DEENSS-*taahk*)
Wednesday	Mittwoch (MIT-*vohk*)
Thursday	Donnerstag (DONN-*er-staahk*)
Friday	Freitag (FRIY-*taahk*)
Saturday	Samstag (ZAHMSS-*taahk*)
Sunday	Sonntag (ZON-*taahk*)
Today	heute (HOY-*te*)
Yesterday	gestern (GHEST-*ern*)
Tonight	heute Abend (HOY-*te* AAH-*bent*)
Tomorrow	morgen (MORRG-*en*)
Week	woche (VOKH-*eg*)
Month	monat (MOH-*naht*)
Year	jahr (YAAHR)

NUMBERS

One	Eins (IYN)
Two	Zwei (TSVIY)
Three	Drei (DRIY)
Four	Vier (FEER)
Five	Fünf (FUNF)
Six	Sechs (ZEKS)
Seven	Sieben (ZEE-*ben*)
Eight	Acht (AHKHT)
Nine	Neun (NOYN)
Ten	Zehn (TSEHN)

MONEY

Money	Geld (GHELT)
Mark	(MAHRK)
Pfennig	(*pfenn-ik*)

INDEX